Redemption Songs

Annie Wright

For Joyce,
love the books you're
doing yourself,
Annie
29/4/03

ARROWHEAD
PRESS

First published 2003 by:
Arrowhead Press
70 Clifton Road, Darlington,
Co. Durham, DL1 5DX
Tel: (01325) 260741

Typeset in Haarlemmer MT - 11 pt
by:
Arrowhead Press

Email: editor@arrowheadpress.co.uk
Website: http://www.arrowheadpress.co.uk

Printed by
Athenaeum Press Gateshead.

Arrowhead Press acknowledges the
financial assistance of Northern Arts.

Acknowledgements

Some of the poems in this book have appeared in or on the following:-

Northern Grit (Vane Women Press)
The Haiku Hundred (Iron Press)
Short and Sweet (Penguin)
Postcards (Vane Women Press)
Tees Valley Writer
Smith's Knoll
A Feather Behind The Ear (Vane Women Press)
Off The Shelf (Vane Women Press)
Vane Women Word Web (website)
Agenda

Coming Home was written for a performance
of *Journey To The West* by Tara Arts

A Marriage won the Yorkshire Prize in the
Yorkshire Open Poetry Competition

for my mother, Ida
and in memory of my father, Colin

Contents

The Night Is Holding Its Breath

I gaze into the pond, wander over the grass
to the apple tree, before I realise I've not breathed.
I let it out, a telltale trail on chill air,
afraid it might be discovered, bagged,
assigned a code and used in evidence.
Trying to be normal, not to arouse suspicion,
I am eaten up with fear. I lean against
the firm back of the apple tree. It upholds me,
lightly, easily, unjudgingly. It does not harm
or bully me, blackmail or provoke. It does not
resent me, hate me or condemn.
It demands nothing from me, although it could,
as I stand here looking for stars, taking its support.
Through its upthrust arms I saw the comet,
heard the urgent message to flee.
I have climbed, hugged and harvested this tree.
Now your new leaves tremble as I say goodbye;
tomorrow, when I've run, it's you I'm going to miss.

American Book Center, Amsterdam

Unmistakably you, that tender patch
of skin below your eye arrests me. Years
of squinting at St Lucian skies have heaped
like lunar dust a purpling slope, fist-rest,
ripe for a lover's kiss. You lean back watchful
warrior, eyes honed on truth beyond the lens,
  rumour without any echo
impassioned muse, the sting of that caress.

The posters aren't for sale, they're just on loan.
I've also tried, the male assistant sighs
and glances coyly up at Donna Tartt.
He's young and sweet, a freshman in his lust,
too inexperienced to guess or trace
those secret histories etched upon the face.

Three Things
(after Anna Akhmatova)

Three things enchanted her:

the sea by moonlight, barefoot
the sound of water trickling in a building
the scent of Opium or her baby's skin

She did not care for
angry voices in a room
instruction manuals
bright orange, mustard and lime green

and she untied herself from him

The Persistence Of Memory

Somewhere
on the edge of memory
I have known him
can smell the good tweed
of a second best, over-worn
jacket where old man
odours cling between the warp
and weft of dull brown fibres.

He has sat next to me on buses
transport to or from unremarkable
destinations, has pressed his thigh
close to mine in the seedy plush
of cinemas, the crush of commuter
trains. I have felt his trembling
fingers spider the distance in the dark
from his territory into mine.

I have seen how he knots his tie
too tight under a stubbled Adam's apple.
Never, even in dreams, have I seen
his eyes. Always below a brim
or averted. The more I try to focus
the more he slips the screen
fading in an insubstantial haze,
dots, oddments, russet leaves, a path,
a tomb, barbed wire or utility sofas.

I never speak. I think he might have spoken
a century ago, but I couldn't understand
the broken words, do not know even
if it was English. He is everyone's great
grandfather, or bogeyman. Someone must
have been hoist upon that knee and jounced,
or not.

Ascending The Bell Tower

When we stop in niches, fumble for mouths,
no-one sees our stolen kisses. I follow,
up, up, charged to remember the precise feel
of good blue cotton, your dark
mouth-cave, cold rancour of recent pasts.

Slit, hooded eyes frown down on prison insects
trudging perimeter, clockwise circles.
Not one crosses pristine, geometric grass
or notices the emerald scent of spring.
Not one casts a glance at the huge bird
hovering

Cars dance in bee formation
at the hive's entrance.
Shrive me, shrive me!
How can you, when I will not repent?
We spiral back on ourselves.
From the gizzard we are vomited out,
pellets of skin, bone, hair,
onto a square roof, unbearable lightness.

My stomach lurches. *Breathe,* you say,
don't look, breathe.
On the narrow ledge I'm reassembled,
my bones spun sugar,
the grey shell cracked.

I unhook from the parapet,
test the four corners of the known world,
temple, tower block, prison, angel.
Angel, angel, truly I am
in the company of angels, o love, love, extend
hubristic wings,
watch me stream in the firmament, follow me
flying, winging, sinning, jubilant, home!

The Bat Moth

I do not know the small cupboard
but I open it.
A chrysalis I could crush in my fist
hangs from the shelf.

A bat-moth is hatching:
it unfurls moleskin wings,
a head grotesquely big,
alluring and malevolent.

The thing clings to the edge.
Now it thrums with life
and the one pure deed, clean as a knife,
I cannot do.

I could have killed it
I tell myself,
while it was encased,
perfectly quiet and still.

Hoping it does not sense my fear,
for its face is yours,
I stand in the closed doorway,
switch off the light.

It launches a titanic flight
across the darkened kitchen,
strikes the opposite wall
and drops, a fallen crucifix.

Grey blood floods the kitchen floor,
pulse after pulse after pulse,
smooth as a lake of cream
it smells of vomit.

Your face looks up at me.
As each gasp for breath
pushes the last blood out
you are begging me,

but I can no more stand
on wet fur, claw and bone
than I can condone.
You die staring at me.

Grey guilt silts my bones,
my mouth a dry slit.
In doing, saying, nothing,
I have condemned, I am condemned.

Every Woman Adores A Fascist

oh it's true, it's true,
at first it seduces, the power,
the charm, that arrogant view,
disregard for the rules
and a voice improbably cool.

before long we school
our thoughts to please you
the shepherdless ewes
you assume have no views
worth listening to

soulless as steel
you apparently feel
merely strength or rage,
a barred cage
conceals what's real

and still we fall
at the fort of your walls
our uniform shirts
conceal the hurt
pretending your actions aren't cruel

penned as lovers or wives
you ramraid our lives
with obedience and duty
kill off unfulfilled beauty
with your lies, lies and damned lies

you exact terrible dues
we're left with the bruise
a black black eye
cries itself dry
you use, use and abuse

but there's a price to pay
for roughshod ways
the colossal statue
has been sawn through
old lies are losing their sway

every woman's a conspirator too
our voices grow stronger with truth
your strategy's rumbled
your citadels tumble
you are lonely and ageing and nude

the unlooked-for denouement
that knife through the suit
cuts deepest when it's she
you thought shackled to you
et tu, et tu, et tu

the reign of terror's done
flowers bloom from the gun
what you imposed
has been exposed
the dawn will bring gentler sons

autumn hacks up leaves
consumptively, glitter-eyed
her bare ribs protrude

▌▌september

today
the topless towers
burned and toppled
over and over
ashen-faced
we saw them fall

we saw them
      f
       a
        l
        l
      in
         g
from the walls
black ants hurt
      l
      i
      n
      g
embracing death
before death

in the belly
of our planes
the enemy came
with deadly cunning
unknown assassins
breached the walls

vertebra
  on
ver te bra
the backbone collapses
cry for the towers
that will never
be raised

shrouded in dust
numb
as numberless lost
scatter as ash
eclipsing hope
even as we choke
on our dead

Redemption Song

What possessed those men of terror
to make their last demands?
There are no absolutes in this world, even such evil.
They too were someone's son, someone's husband,
someone's loving father once.

Not sure how long was left
and no rehearsal,
so many tiny messages of love.

Love you always

Tell mom

If I don't make it

Tell the kids I love them

Honey I may not come back

Float their last words in paper boats
down all the rivers
of this still beautiful world.

This is the poignant victory
love still triumphing
in text messages
on mobile phones
on answerphones
endlessly replayed

Honey I may not

           Tell the kids

     If I don't

               Tell mom

   Always

        Always

                  Love

              Love

                        Love

Rain At Midnight

The wettest April for a hundred years
has woken me, is crying all our tears
and I, dry-eyed, still can't believe I won't
see you again or listen to your jokes.
I need to sense a shiver in the room,
something to reassure me you're not gone,
but all that flickers is my starfish child,
your only grandson, stranded by my side.

Outside, the teeming pulse of rain on roads,
unbearable reminder that your throat
dried up, the man of patter silenced.
I replay final moments to the end.
The dreamer in my bed lets out a sigh
and all that's risen to my throat subsides.

Easter Lilies At Salt's Mill

Those flowers you knew I'd craved in Amsterdam,
that curled and posed in windows by canals
provocative as prostitutes or cats,
then lay as stiff as corpses in my hands.
The pallor of their faces chilled my breath.
Your birthday gift to me. I found a vase
to fill the void where once we would have spoken.
For weeks the backroom reeked of funerals.

Today the lilies are a resurrection,
pure white angelic trumpets oozing jazz
and sultry scent, among the canvases
a bigger splash. Yellow stamens burst
with Hockney's Californian light, spilling
it over Saltaire, Bradford, England, me.

Jameela

I missed the subtleties of idiom,
stumbled over basics, *how much?*
where is? too hot! - needed definition,
communication of something more than
trivialities. A bird of prey wheeled
endlessly. *What is it? Da shinuu?* I asked.
Bird Mohammed replied.
Yes bird, but what kind?
Mohammed didn't know, it wasn't edible.
Abdul, the driver, understood.
It was an eagle, in Arabic shohgar.
One day a bird no bigger than a finch,
glossy black with bright vermilion vest,
flitted through a millet field. *Da shinuu?*
They were used to this by now.
Shohgar said Mohammed proudly.
I discerned two names for the moon,
learned that at this farthest point in Africa
from coast and tides, a further twenty-seven
had eluded me. Mercury sweated in the forties,
the sun forged leaner, keener blades of us.
Abu arrar, the village elders called it,
father of axes. I smiled, for once I'd understood.
They smiled. *Come we want to show you something.*
Wanting the town's cool water, shade, I trudged
through stinging sand towards the wadi.
Nothing to see there.
Women dredging up water, nomads in the distance,

habitual donkeys, children playing,
black kites circling overhead.
No no, they urged, *here*, gesturing down.
On parched, fissured earth a bed of waterlilies
shimmered, waxy, white. No lake, no mirage.
Jameela, beautiful! I shrieked
and raced to breathe their perfume.
Dancing round pads of green like camels' feet,
tracing tough ropes that linked the saddle packs
of blooms, I heard the elders braying,
knew that sometimes subtleties don't matter.

a bitter morning:
ice on the path
where his car
did not return

Short Fuse

this month explodes in gold
brilliantly upstaging
faded April's creams and blues

dandelions galaxy the verges
each star fizzling
on its own short fuse

electric rape
dynamites the senses
detonates swarms

I slough layers
towards a white gold core
I smile at strangers

sing to sheep warming up
by coppery gorse, remember
how you exploded inside

me eleven Mays ago
and I spent days
tasting rawness

you will be surprised that
shining throats of kingcups
remind me of you

not your favourite colour
but I am driving fast wanting
your dangerous gold charge

Paradoxically Speaking

There is total truth in the rumour,
the dead have not fallen asleep,
Liverpool's no sense of humour,
there's no telling goats from sheep.

The poor inherited poverty,
the rich will inherit a lot more,
if theft's your way into property
you won't be shown the door.

Wise virgins abandoned housework
since the risen Lord hadn't risen,
he who laughed first still smirks,
the fact of the matter isn't.

The future looks set to be male,
the camera frequently lies,
what you don't know hurts like hell,
the cherries are gone from pies.

Black holes are lighting the universe
and traffic wardens are kind,
things can and will get worse,
we're all of us in the wrong mind.

A Marriage

This metal when it fractures will not mend.
Welded at the head, she is the fixed
foot that rips and gouges square-ruled books.
She'd like to turn her vicious tip on him,
but scoring points only shreds her paper
heart to dust. He is the dancing foot,
dangling redundant as an ankle clip
without a cyclist. Where one inclined,
the other leaned in tango. Now she complains
he leads the dance with her forever in
his wake. He believes she checks his orbit,
limiting his scope. The further apart
they tug, the more their circles waver.
Both dream of intersecting other arcs.

Not An Important Day

Not the Prophet's birthday,
no special visitors due,
so you were granted

honorary woman's status.
Men withdrew, bemused,
from the Furshur's kitchen.

Zamzam, his number two wife,
teased and tugged grey hair,
called you *shaiba* – old woman.

Spearing titbits from the pot
she proffered them around
ordered you to chop the onions.

Hawa, Asha and Feday ran
cackling up the path,
set the hens off squawking:

smothered you with hugs and grins,
fast-spat up your arms for luck,
abandoned concealing robes.

Hunkered round the charcoal fire,
howling, hooting, that day
we drank our tea before the men.

Sucking the bitter syrup
they asked about your son,
why we had no children,

whether (pointed looks and sniggers)
we shared the same hut at night,
who you wanted for your number two.

Once you looked up,
saw dangling from the rafters
the sheep's penis and balls.

Chaos Theory

Did you know the confused, amorphous mass
that was me, eddying and swirling in currents
of scorn, was a desperate cry for order
when I doubted its very existence?

Did you know my unpredictability
when I hurled the paint tin, clawed your face,
was only apparently random behaviour
within a rigid, determinist system?

Did you know when you called me butterfly
for evading your pinning down,
of the effect the mere flap of a wing could have,
the difference between a hurricane striking

or not?

december trees

flamenco dancers
bony limbs decked in black lace
such frosty eyed flirts

Anyone's Eyes

Perhaps today. At three he makes tea,
the unused pot a dull reminder.
He spoons sugar, blows the surface.

I am forty-eight years old and
I live alone. Smoke Os ripple out.
I am lonely and would like
a boy to love and care for
in my home.

Other tenants' dramas invade
his rubbish chute. He practises smiling,
slicks back a lick of hair,
slides the comb into his pocket.

I like boys of about sixteen years of age
with blond hair, blue eyes and smooth
bodies, who I can hold in my arms and love
and watch them while they sleep.

The stone stairs reek of poverty and piss.
On Kennington Road he crosses at the lights.
Five to. He waits. Kids snigger and point.
He lights up. Sticks and stones.
They run away. Perhaps today.

I like cocks of every size. He steps down.
A man streams a steady arc, he manages
a trickle, checks the mirror. *I am here*
every day between four and six o'clock.

Men come and go. No-one speaks. He shivers.
Cold seeps from the tiles. He can't catch
anyone's eyes. Smoke rings disintegrate
like wreaths. He smiles. *Please leave*
a number or make a date to meet me.

Star Man
(A version after Estrela Da Manha by Manuel Bandeira)

I might as well ask for a man from the stars
Where's there a star who's a man?
My friend my inimitable boy
Procure me a star of a man

Alas she is in despair but have you never
Been in despair like this?
Procure for my spirits a part of him

I don't give a sous for um, a man who handles his love organ
But ah, a man who attends to her pudenda
Do you get my meaning?
I really am asking for an extra-terrestrial man

Three days and three nights
Since I was assassinated by him and suicidal
Jack the Lad, puller, betrayer

A woman so unlucky in love
I bring down on him twin afflictions
Stretch his knackers like giraffe-necks
I have sinned for a drink I have sinned with drunks

I've peccadilloed with bad lads
I've tinkered with sergeants
Fossicked with fusiliers, navvies
I've copped off on the job with manual workers
With Greeks and with Trojans
With the priest and with the choirboy
With the leper from Chicken Alley

I have mixed them all up like peas

My hope for you with your broadsword my newest cavalier
     circle the earth and direct the chosen one to my womb
     a consummation devoutly simple
That you will commit to my crusade

Procure him for my soul even a particle
An innocent undefiled, edible, the ultimate sixpack
So hard
        I am longing
              for a man
                     who is out of this world

between the pages
of a favourite book I find
squashed fruit-cake crumbs

Driving Urge

When I see you eye
motorbikes outside supermarkets
or wriggle from your child restraint
so by the time I've climbed out
and walked round to the passenger door
you're eeled into the driver's seat
steering, flicking wipers, lights and switches
delight and power in your eyes
I'm scared

I know
I want to wrench you from the wheel
to clutch you desperately tight
in the airbag of my arms
to kiss your one-and-three-quarter
year old curls and steer you
from machines, high speeds, the thrills
that, ill-fated, I'm even now
too late to quell

Geography Of A Woman

Sunlight on water dapples the shadows.
Words ripple the surface of an open book
whose pages might let me enter
if I could click their language,
the rhythm of their dipthongs, gunfire
consonants. Laze instead
below the barbarous curve of hills,
sacred barrows where they buried
arrows, spear tips, precious metal;
the grave goods of hunter warriors.
This afternoon is camouflaged,
the skin of a gazelle,
a trompe l'oeil of darting patterns, roads
not taken, the flinty dazzle of light on axe
blades, a sea of waves, unfathomable as
this languid moment, this book, this woman.

Heartsease

Here in the white house
in the white rooms
in the stripped down
bones of the place
there is a white so white
at first it hurts then soothes
clean as a pebble.

Here in the farthest North I've ever been
the days are mild
the winds a warm bath
nights balmy with stars
and absurd conversation,
the sort you'd have with Death
were he to turn up invited.

Here there is a casting off
of the old hurts,
a trawling down
to a deeper catch,
and in the morning
the gift of a small garden flower
easing the heart.

My Father Dying
(after Untitled, 1969 by Mark Rothko)

There is a moment

when the sugar pinks of afternoon
spun almost out of existence
gleam brittle bright

when evening's grey skirt
swirls and rustles
a pearl bloom on its silk

when dull mauve is transfigured
heliotroped and breathing
a shimmering miracle

as if one dead or dying metaphor
juxtaposed with living death
was charged with vibrant meaning

he confronts us with this moment
of stillness, a canvas vast as
the pathways of the mind

and this lie, as though there is
a possibility of pink,
grey receding to an ash speck

whereas you slip so imperceptibly
from pink to mauve
a gradual suffusion of grey

your lips a no-man's land
plumb exit line
from flesh to spirit

that you have already seeped
into the masked-off edge
of white surrender

before I realise

Why I Kept My Father's Shirt

Because it was soft textured, warm to touch,

because it wasn't stiffly ironed, on the pile
laid out for British Heart or Age Concern,

because it was heathery, moorland colours,
because the collar was starting to fray,

because it would come in useful for decorating,
because I'd wanted to be an artist or a potter,

because it would always be too big,

because he wore it in the Ruby Wedding photo
snapped in the Autumn woods outside my home,

because I could keep it in the airing cupboard,
because it almost held the scent of him,

because mauve was the colour of my grief,

because, as his eldest, it was time
to don his mantle, step into his shoes.

autumn lesson – fall
in love with poetry, not
an ardent poet

Poem Card Haiku

shuffle if you choose

my poem cards make sense of
love's bleak treacheries

a lacquered wood box

gold chrysantheum arching
between stippled breasts

starkly black and white

honesty by the mirror
no reflected face

a snake or two fish

wise sensitivity or
reckless union

in the carved bed's bliss

the carpenter's dovetails and
the poet's couplings

I'm half a poem

inexplicable sadness
unfinished poet

you may never know

the poet's true intention
is this my result?

(Inspired by a Japanese game dating from the 16th century whose object was to match cards depicting poetesses and the first halves of their poems correctly with the second halves.)

The Woman Who

I am the woman
who put chocolate stars on the head of Buddha
who was swept up in a comet's dust trail
who tracked a UFO's arc across Highland skies
then learned it was a satellite
who reburied the cat when stiff grey paws poked through
I am a torn blind dancer on a rip-up by Matisse

I am the woman
who danced with Sky Eagle and fathered Little Bear
who kicked red maple leaves to stars
turned stars to floating leaves
who saw yesterday's knickers slip from her jeans
who sought her muse in a graveyard
I am O'Keeffe's morning glory rubbing up black petunia

I am the rippling arpeggios of an indoor fountain
the warning stroke of the scirocco
I am the hot eruption of purple
the cool of lapis lazuli or any Callas aria
know me by my bell, books and candles
you will never exorcise me

Toad

My flashlight picks him out
among the pitchers of water hyacinth
serenading mournfully
forget-me-not, an open-throated
aria. He floats, fingers splayed,
leg trailing in a dancer's pose.
Harsh yellow lights a mottled belly:
age spots and leathery chins belie his youth.

Hapless gigolo. The slow
blink of your umber eyes is not enough.
Two fat and fed-up female tourists
attempt to lose the mob of bottom-pinchers,
their jostling, ducking braggadocio.
You elsewhere, on a bridge of sighs,
goggle at an artificial moon,
lonesome tenor, my wishful crooner.

Anemones 1916
(after Charles Rennie Mackintosh)

bringing false hope of Spring to a dull
interior. Full-skirted bella donnas,
fragile dark eyes, our ladies, ladies
of the night, high on laudanum,
rouged with consumptive flushes,
you dance on purest ether.

Like a mother I arrange you in glorious swathes,
admire your coming out in perfect bloom,
want to preserve this glittering fragment for ever,
gloss over the papery rattle in your throats.
I see you obsessed as anorexics,
translucent ivory thinning to blue.

Belles whose evanescent beauty only an addicted,
dying architect could capture, tomorrow
your gorgeous skirts will flag, your limbs
will droop, you'll lie heavy-eyed, weary,
spent, lolling over the ebony table,
ominous red petals spilt on tar.

Sweetheart

Red was our secret.
Those cards with red hearts sent
each Valentine's, that I, red-faced at school,
pretended were from some red-faced
spotty youth I didn't care for. I wanted red
red roses, satin hearts, red ribbons, all
the clichéd stuff, but from some red-blooded
Romeo, whom I, blushing furious red, could
confess to staining my sheets red with.

Passion's much like embarrassment, it's red
and easily misread, red-hot, molten,
uncontrollable. It leads to red-rimmed eyes,
emotions overdrawn, a balance tipped into the red.

The boys and men I was red hot for
never understood the barbed red hints and arrows
stupid Cupid, pouting red lips, misfired.
Your disguised writing, the same squiggly red
with big red biro question mark – *guess who?* – plopped
unfailingly on the mat each year. Your red hearts
stopped after I married and I stopped going red
defending your sweetheart gesture. Red's
the colour of betrayal; to my red shame
I was never grateful. Now your red heart's
stopped, I'd give up shopfuls of red roses
for that one card signed in red – *guess who?*

On St. Valentine's Day

Where were you? You must have sent a card
although it wouldn't have arrived on time.
A perfect night for love, for massacre,
under a perfect lovers'/bombers' moon,
I like to think it was the date you asked her.
Wartime romance, the surging drone, it's hard
to picture what they felt during the climb
avenging Coventry by bombing Dresden.

Fires consuming cities and two hearts
exchanged in Middlesbrough at the fireman's ball,
destructive evidence of Europe's crimes.
Two cities that have been rebuilt in parts,
a union that still holds me in its thrall
though you're consumed by fire this final time.

beach in summer

shorn sheep on the cliffs –
shivering in bathers, wishing
we'd brought fleeces

The Poetry Of Pool

Squaring up to the green I took my cue
from you, rattled balls in the three line frame,
jostling thoughts on an empty page while you

promised to teach me how to play the game.
I used the chalk, practised taking a shot.
Break like one thought, you cued. I did the same

and saw the white dislodge a single spot,
a stirring like our look across a room,
idea forming needing you to pot

it. *Yeah, that's good,* you told me through the gloom,
you've got the first verse off to a clean start.
We sat together, let a rhythm loom.

The other team criss-crossed a random chart
of stripes for stars, while yours and mine danced a
lambada, hot minimalists at heart.

My turn. *Just think of this as a stanza
break.* You on form, I gave the white a whack
and took the pot ending snookered, hands a

kimbo. The cannon weighing on my back
you sprung my rhythm, *Give your hip some sway.*
I loosened up until the final black,

that full stop missed, you kissed my black away.

Rock Scissors Paper

Rock blunts
Scissors cut
Paper wraps

One two three
Jacob produces paper
a fraction after
my fist and wins.

You have to play fair
I say. *No, I have to win.*

My voice takes on a gravel
edge. I instruct him in rules
for playing clean. I too
like winning. He frowns at
my cliff face. On a sudden
count of three we both
show fists.

His eyes are flinty
chips, he is used to
winning. One two three
he pulls out scissors –
so do I. He growls
all his double three years
in that scowl.

I offer a hug. Who'd want
a hug with me
all my craggy side
still showing? Around me
the kitchen's covered in paper
messages and hearts
I love you mummy xxx

Millstone grit is crumbling.
Jacob has a cuddle,
counts to three. We're grinning
as paper greets paper.
No win I say.

Look he says joining
the edge of our hands,
papers arching from
a shared spine,
we've made a book.

Crossing Over
(i.m. Howard Stuart Smith)

water, your element
constant struggle against
a downstream mind

you on the canal bank
saying *'ow do – owt doing?*
to all the fishermen

baiting your line with
bovril, spam, maggots,
eating tuna sandwiches

too impatient for
the gentle carp
the deadly snap of pike

landing perch, tench,
roach, you reel in
wildly, exotic dancer

they flap absurdly
you have to ask your dad
to disgorge them

today he casts five
teacakes, two reels, yours
and his, into the water

I throw in two two-pence
pieces for the fare –
you were always broke –

ready for the boatman
to hook you, gently as
your dad reeling in

On The Road

Hey crazy Jack, is this what happens
after all, clapped out in a field mid-West,
mid-North, mid-life, having gone
for juice, for caffeine, dope, those highs
that rocketed the fuel of being twenty one
with all our young life surging forward, fast-laning
it up the back end of trucks and jerks
who heard the honks, saw on-off lights and pulled
back mid-average-lane, so flashing past
we revved it up down all the sweet
M-ways of our futures, and making it,
o baby making it, fast and bitter as
slugged coffee, untipped smokes, reckless rides?

I guess one day we ran out of juice,
somewhere in a field and heading North
in my case, though a body still embodies a dream
that if I could hack this bracken forest back
I might recall what it was, why it haunts
me now; it's not so crazy, the shift
stick still shifts, the dash could take
a takeaway coffee, cappuccino to go,
in styrofoam – it nettles me, it nettles, so
now I've glimpsed it, I'm fighting not
to let it hole up here for good,
o crazy Jack, is it absolutely crazy
to cherish still the dream
of getting the whole, unbelievable thing
out there, out and flying, freewheeling on the road again?

I want to open
like the teahouse
walls, reveal my
still fragrant hearth

Full Moon Over Manjushri

The moon a silken prayer wheel centred
over the temple of peace, perfect, whole.
Driving back, cats' eyes pick out the curved
wall, saffron set in eerie limestone.
Car headlamps bounce off the bronze
buck, *bliss*, easy to miss.
I'm missing the doe, *emptiness*.

You with the photographer's eye for odd
light, jumping from the car
two hours ago, caught pallido oro,
late December's washed out plum clouds.
Me later, gleaning details from lit windows
of closed estate agents; as usual, dreaming
another life, that golden place, perfect, whole.

Resting Place

After 200 wearisome years of being bumped, jogged and dumped
the length and breadth of the true North,
up and down the old A1, across the Pennine Way
coast to unending coast, Cuthbert's bones had had enough.
From Lindisfarne to Kelso, Edinburgh to Ormesby, Cockermouth
to York by way of Darlington and Ripon, there's a limit
to the number of churches one wants raised in one's name.
The worms long since given up and gone, all he wanted
was cessation, deep eternal rest for profoundly weary bones.
But how to signal this to clerics whose lifetime pilgrimage
was this? No place apparently *the* place to call a final halt.

Today trees that might be great great grandchildren of saplings
Cuthbert's bones passed by, tower loftily,
shimmer gold leaf on the Wear below the loftier,
impossibly man-made towers of the cathedral,
built where his bones refused to budge. As mine would,
as mine, had I all this to remain within forever –
resting-place that, in this moment, upstages heaven.

Windchime

I am the Emperor's serving maid.
Dink he says, pointing
teetering in tiny slippers
and thus it becomes dink, it is decreed.
Sometimes in quiet contemplation
I stumble across him at his devotions.
Dink he says, inclining his head, *dink-k-k-k-k.*
It is the clinking of wind through the clapper,
the staccato patter of sparrows' feet
taking off from the almond tree,
the echoing *ring-k-k-k* of tubes in a lift of air.
Dink he commands, pointing imperiously.
Dutifully I dink it, making it dink.
His lifted head widens in a beatific grin.
Yesterday I held him in my upstretched arms
so he could dink. We laughed and laughed,
he dinked and dinked
until our laughter too became the dink.

Zen Walking

Rising early and walking in the garden
I slip off my shoes. The lawn's a cold plunge.
The soles of my feet wake up.

My son is fretting at my skirt.
Yesterday he walked. Today
he wants a carry.

Can I walk in the garden
barefoot, mindful of each footfall,
each full breath and carry him?

Lifting him, thumb in mouth
he pours his slumbering weight
into the bowl of me,

and now, the earth beneath
chill grass a warm surprise;
it is baked Alaska inside out.

As I think of breathing
in, left foot, out, right foot,
his head is rising and falling

in time with my measured
pace. We are two and one, and so
it was when I carried him.

Our Buddhist guide sounds the singing bowl.
We stop, look up. In the stillness
a ripe pear drops.

Coming Home

When your solicitor asks
what you want doing
with your remains, he said,
it kind of stops you in your tracks.
It stopped me.

He said, *Scatter my ashes*
in mid-Atlantic. Home the exact
mid-point of triangular diaspora,
West Africa, West Indies, West
Yorkshire. Latterly New York.

What do I want doing
with mine?
I've no more sense
of belonging anywhere,
though two years in Sudan
had me grieving for
the sound of water.

Scatter my ashes
in the river Colden
a point equidistant
from Lumb Mill chimney
and The New Delight.

Water, my element too,
under a lowering sky
black silk river, garrulous
and grumbling in widows'
weeds, somewhere you can
never step in twice;
home, that's about
as close as I get.